DOOMED HISTORY

DEATH AT THE SOUTH POLE!

Antarctica, 1911-1912

by Nancy Dickman

BEARPORT
PUBLISHING

Minneapolis, Minnesota

Picture Credits: Front Cover, ©Danvis Collection/Alamy; 1, Scott's Last Expedition/R.F. Scott/Public Domain; 3, The South Pole/John Murray, London 1913/Olav Bjaaland/ Public Domain; 5, Alexander Turnball National Library/Herbert Ponting/Public Domain; 6, ©Sean M Smith/Shutterstock; 7, Bonhams/Herbert Ponting/Public Domain; 8, ©LouieLea/ Shutterstock; 9, National Library of NZ/Herbert Ponting/Public Domain; 10, ©NASA/Joe Macgregor; 11, Christie's/Herbert Ponting/ Public Domain; 12, Scott's Last Expedition/R.F. Scott/Public Domain; 13, ©The History Collection/Alamy; 14, ©goinyk/iStock; 15, ©The Print Collector/Alamy; 16, ©New Africa/Shutterstock; 17, ©Archive Pics/Alamy; 18, ©Robert Mcgillivray/Shutterstock; 19, Alexander Turnball National Library/Herbert Ponting/ Public Domain; 20–21, ©The Print Collector/Alamy; 22, ©Benoit Rousseau/iStock; 23, ©Abbus Acastra/Alamy; 24, Scott Polar Research Institute Cambridge/Herbert Ponting/Public Domain; 25, Bonhams/Herbert Ponting/Public Domain; 26–27 ©barneygumble/Public domain; 28, ©Jeremy Richards/Shutterstock; 29, ©penguinFR/ Shutterstock.

Bearport Publishing Company Product Development Team
President: Jen Jenson; Director of Product Development: Spencer Brinker; Senior Editor: Allison Juda; Editor: Charly Haley; Associate Editor: Naomi Reich; Senior Designer: Colin O'Dea; Associate Designer: Elena Klinkner; Product Development Assistant: Anita Stasson

Brown Bear Books
Children's Publisher: Anne O'Daly; Design Manager: Keith Davis;
Picture Manager: Sophie Mortimer

Library of Congress Cataloging-in-Publication Data is available at www.loc.gov or upon request from the publisher.

ISBN: 979-8-88509-082-7 (hardcover)
ISBN: 979-8-88509-089-6 (paperback)
ISBN: 979-8-88509-096-4 (ebook)

For more information, write to Bearport Publishing, 5357 Penn Avenue South, Minneapolis, MN 55419. Printed in the United States of America.

CONTENTS

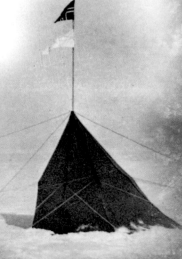

INTO THE UNKNOWN

Five men stood shivering in the icy wind and blinding snow.

Two months earlier, a large group of explorers, led by Robert Falcon Scott, had started out from their base on the Antarctic coast. Their goal was to reach the South Pole. As they got closer, Scott began sending some team members back to **base camp** to pick up supplies that would be needed for their return journey. On January 4, he sent the last of these support groups back to camp. Scott and four remaining team members planned to make the final push to the pole. But they would never be seen alive again.

Race to the Pole

In Scott's time, the South Pole was one of the world's last unexplored places. Reaching it meant walking hundreds of miles across Antarctica's frozen wasteland. It took months, and explorers had to carry enough supplies for the entire journey. Several had tried and failed. In 1911, two teams set off on a race to the pole. Scott led the British team. The other was a Norwegian team led by Roald Amundsen. Who would get there first?

Scott was a captain in the British Navy. He was chosen to lead a group to the South Pole.

THE FIRST SIGNS OF TROUBLE

One year earlier, Scott's ship had landed on the Antarctic coast after a difficult journey.

The rough seas around Antarctica are filled with floating blocks of ice. It had taken Scott's ship, the *Terra Nova*, three weeks to ram through the icy waters and reach the frozen **continent**. It was now summer in Antarctica, though the temperature rarely rose above freezing. Scott's team quickly built a large hut. Winter would bring constant darkness and even colder temperatures.

The rough wooden hut provided shelter for about two dozen men and their supplies.

Scott's ponies came from northeastern China. They were used to cold weather.

Scott's Plan

Scott planned to use the next several months to haul supplies. His team would leave them in **depots** along the route to the pole. That way, when the journey began, they would have less to carry. They could refill their supplies from the depots along the way. Scott had ponies, dogs, and even a few motorized sleds. But his men would end up doing most of the sled-pulling themselves.

The Journey Begins

Scott gave the order to begin the journey to the South Pole on October 24, 1911. The first group headed out with the motorized sleds. But the machines broke down shortly after they left. The sleds now had to be pulled by hand. Still, the men soon settled into a daily routine of breakfast, breaking camp, and trudging south before setting up the next camp. On a good day, they might cover 15 miles (25 km).

The first part of Scott's journey took him across a giant sheet of ice more than 1,100 feet (335 m) thick.

Going Wrong

The loss of the motorized sleds was a big setback. Even worse, the team's ponies were struggling in the cold and snow. Several died. That meant there weren't enough animals to pull all the sleds. The weather was bad, too. First they had to travel through heavy snow. Then, a slushy thaw made the journey even harder.

Scott's motorized sleds ran on **gasoline** and had tracks, like a tank.

SCOTT'S EXPEDITION

The British team that set off for the South Pole in October 1911 included
* 16 men
* 10 ponies
* 23 sled dogs
* 13 regular sleds
* 2 motorized sleds
* More than a ton of food and camping supplies

The team led by Amundsen had only 5 men, 4 sleds, and no ponies. However, he had 52 sled dogs, and his team included excellent skiers.

Getting Closer

By December 21, there were just eight men left in Scott's team. The rest had been sent back to base camp, along with the remaining dogs. All the ponies were now dead. Scott was still more than 300 miles (480 km) from the pole, and there were no more supply depots ahead of them. It was up to him and his men to drag everything they needed on their sleds.

Scott's team had a difficult trek along the rough surface of the Beardmore **Glacier**.

THE FINAL FIVE

Scott himself led the final group. It included Edward Wilson, his chief scientist, and Lawrence Oates, an army officer. Edgar Evans was chosen for his strength. Henry Bowers, known as "Birdie," was added at the last minute because of his skills as a navigator.

Wilson was respected by his team. They nicknamed him "Uncle Bill."

Change of Plans

Scott's original plan was for four men to make the final push. But at the last minute, he decided five would continue to the pole. This ended up causing problems. The team now had extra pulling power but not enough food or fuel. Scott had calculated his supplies based on a four-man team.

DISASTER STRIKES

Hungry and tired, Scott and his team were closing in on the South Pole. Then, they saw something that made their hearts sink.

It was "Birdie" Bowers who spotted it first—a black flag flapping in the wind. They drew closer and found paw prints and dog waste in the surrounding snow. This meant that the Norwegians had reached the pole first! Scott was very disappointed. He had been convinced that they were in the lead. But Amundsen's team had followed a different route, so there had been no sign of them until the very end.

Amundsen's team had reached the South Pole on December 14.

Bowers attached a string to a camera to take a selfie of Scott's South Pole team.

The Pole at Last

Scott and his men trudged the last few miles to the Pole. There, they found a Norwegian tent. A date on a letter left by Amundsen showed that he had reached the pole more than a month earlier. Scott's team raised a flag and took photos. They had lost the race to be first. Now, it was a race of a different kind—to get back to the safety of base camp before winter struck.

IN SCOTT'S WORDS

After reaching the pole, Scott wrote in his diary, "The pole. Yes, but under very different circumstances from those expected. We have had a horrible day. . . . Great God! this is an awful place."

13

A Long Journey

Scott's team had a return journey of more than 800 miles (1,300 km) ahead of them. They were going back the same way they had come, so at least they knew the route. That was the only bright side, though. The team members were worn out. Even worse, the Antarctic summer was ending rapidly, and the temperatures were already dropping.

The average January temperature at the South Pole is –18 degrees Fahrenheit (–10 degrees Celcius). By March, that drops to –65°F (–36°C).

Scott's team ate only sugar, butter, biscuits, and a mixture of dried meat and fat called **pemmican**.

Cold and Hungry

Scott and his team needed to make it to the next depot to restock on food. Unfortunately, even this resupply wouldn't be enough to give them the energy they would need to pull the sleds. Scott's men were also getting **dehydrated**, but their fuel supplies were too small to waste on melting snow to drink.

Citrus fruits like limes have plenty of vitamin C. However, Scott's rations didn't contain any.

Health Problems

Scott's men weren't getting enough food, nor were they eating the right kind. All the men developed **scurvy**, a disease caused by a lack of vitamin C. Scurvy leads to tiredness, sore joints, and bleeding gums. It also makes cuts and wounds heal more slowly. The extreme cold was causing **frostbite**. This is when exposed skin and tissues below it freeze and are badly damaged.

Evans's Death

Edgar Evans's health was starting to fail. He had a cut on his hand that would not heal. He was losing weight, and his hands were badly frostbitten. On February 4, he fell into a crack in the ice. He was pulled out, but became even more sick. Then he began to behave strangely, which frightened his teammates. On February 17, he collapsed and died a short time later.

There were now only four men left.

Scott and Evans knew each other well. This was their second Antarctic expedition together.

From Bad to Worse

Evans's health problems had slowed the team down. They were covering less than 10 miles (16 km) a day, and winter was getting worse. Every time they reached a supply depot, they were disappointed by the fuel supplies they found there. They used a liquid fuel called **paraffin** in their stoves. But the **canisters** hadn't been fully sealed, and some of the fuel had escaped in the cold temperatures.

The team sometimes had to stop to shelter from Antarctica's strong winds.

Another Loss

Lawrence Oates felt he was close to dying. An old bullet wound in his leg was hurting badly, thanks to scurvy. Even worse, his feet were so frostbitten that **gangrene** had set in—the flesh had died and turned black. He could barely walk, and he knew that he was slowing the others down. On March 17, he told them, "I am just going out and may be some time." Then, he crawled out of the tent and was never seen again.

LIFE OR DEATH

Only three men remained.
They were still nearly
150 miles (240 km) from the
safety of base camp.

Scott, Wilson, and Bowers were in bad shape. With Evans and Oates dead, there was more food to go around, but it still wasn't enough. The men were starving and losing hope of reaching safety. They stumbled along through the snow, pulling their sleds. Scott's right foot became badly frostbitten, and their progress was slow. Each day brought lower temperatures. Winter was nearly there.

IN SCOTT'S WORDS

The day after Oates's death, Scott wrote in his diary, "The cold is intense, -40°F [-22°C] at midday. My companions are unendingly cheerful, but we are all on the verge of serious frostbites, and though we constantly talk of fetching through [making it to safety], I don't think any one of us believes it in his heart. We are cold on the march now, and at all times except meals. Yesterday, we had to lay up for a **blizzard**, and today we move dreadfully slowly."

Bowers took this photo of their campsite in the shadow of a towering mountain.

Hoping for Rescue

What had kept Scott going was the hope that a team would come out from base camp to rescue them. He hoped to meet a team resupplying one of the depots near their base. Then, they could send for sled dogs at the base to bring the tired and injured men the rest of the way.

Sled dogs have thick fur to protect them from the cold.

Apsley Cherry-Garrard took the dogs to One Ton Depot. He later wrote a book about Scott's expedition.

Unexpected Delays

Back at base camp, Scott's second-in-command became seriously ill with scurvy. The expedition doctor saved him, but he wasn't able to take the dogs south to meet Scott with supplies and aid. He sent two others instead. They made it as far as the One Ton Depot on March 4. They camped there for six days but were snowed in by a blizzard. Then, with no sign of Scott, they left the depot and returned to base.

The Final Camp

By March 21, Scott, Wilson, and Bowers were only 11 miles away from One Ton Depot. They pitched their tent as a furious blizzard blew in. Scott's frostbitten foot left him unable to walk. He knew that even if he survived, his foot would have to be **amputated**. Two days later, Wilson and Bowers planned to leave for the depot to collect supplies and bring them back. But the blizzard was so bad that they had to stay in the tent for shelter.

The *Terra Nova* had been forced to leave Antarctica on March 3 without its full crew. If it had stayed longer, it would have been trapped all winter by ice.

IN SCOTT'S WORDS

Scott's final diary entry was written on March 29. "We are getting weaker, of course, and the end cannot be far. It seems a pity, but I do not think I can write more."

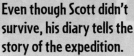
Even though Scott didn't survive, his diary tells the story of the expedition.

The End at Last

As the blizzard raged, the three men used up the last of their food and fuel. They knew there was no hope of survival. Weak and hungry, they spent their final days writing letters to friends and family back home, in the hopes that their bodies would be found one day. They died in their tent at the end of March.

WHAT HAPPENED NEXT

Soon, the darkness of the Antarctic winter settled in. It left the rest of Scott's team stuck at base camp.

For the remaining men, it was a long, cold winter. They knew that Scott and the others—their friends and fellow team members—could not have survived. But they continued their scientific work, and when spring came, they set out see what they could find. It took just over two weeks of retracing their route before one of the men spotted something in the distance. It was Scott's tent, almost completely covered by a **snowdrift**.

Saving History

The men in the search party collected the letters, diaries, rock samples, and photographs from the tent. They left the bodies in the sleeping bags where they had been found and collapsed the tent. On top of it they built a **cairn** out of rocks, topped with a cross made from wooden skis. They spent a moment of silence for the dead. Then, it was time to go home.

The survivors later put up a cross overlooking one of Scott's former bases near the coast.

Leaving His Mark

Although Scott did not survive, he was seen as a hero. He had finally reached the South Pole, even if he hadn't been first. After the news of his death reached London, the king led a memorial service for Scott and his men. Members of the public donated money to help the families of those who had died. Some of the money was also used for polar research.

After his death, Robert Scott was remembered with statues and memorials.

The South Pole Today

Antarctica has now been crossed many times by explorers and adventurers. Scientists from many different countries live and work there. Most research bases are near the coast, so that scientists can easily get to them. But there is one base located at the South Pole. Built in 1956, it includes telescopes and other scientific tools. The base was named the Amundsen-Scott South Pole Station—after the two men who raced there so long ago.

KEY DATES

1910

June 15 Scott's expedition leaves the UK aboard the *Terra Nova*

1911

January 4 The *Terra Nova* lands in Antarctica

October 24 The first group leaves camp for the South Pole

December 14 Roald Amundsen's team reaches the South Pole

1912

January 4 The last support group turns back, leaving Scott and four others

January 17 Scott's team arrives at the South Pole

January 25 Amundsen's team returns safely to their base camp

February 17 Edgar Evans dies

March 17 Lawrence Oates dies

March 19 Scott, Wilson, and Bowers make their final camp

March 29 Scott makes his final diary entry

November 12 The bodies of Scott, Wilson, and Bowers are found

QUIZ

How much have you learned about the South Pole? It's time to test your knowledge! Then, check your answers on page 32.

1. **What was the name of Scott's ship?**
   a. *Endurance*
   b. *Terra Nova*
   c. *Fram*

2. **How many men from Scott's team—including Scott—reached the South Pole?**
   a. 3
   b. 4
   c. 5

3. **Which of these animals did Scott NOT use to haul supplies?**
   a. donkeys
   b. dogs
   c. ponies

4. **What was the first sign that Amundsen's team had reached the Pole first?**
   a. a Norwegian flag
   b. a black flag
   c. an abandoned sled

5. **Which disease is caused by a lack of vitamin C?**
   a. scurvy
   b. diabetes
   c. Covid

GLOSSARY

amputated cut off because a body part is badly damaged

astronomy the scientific study of space and space objects

base camp a camp from which an expedition sets off

blizzard a severe winter storm with heavy snow and strong winds

cairn a mound of stones set up as a landmark or a memorial

canisters containers, usually made of metal, that are used for storing food or chemicals

continent one of the world's seven large land masses

dehydrated having lost a large amount of water from the body

depots places where large quantities of food or supplies are stored

frostbite damage to the body's skin and tissues caused by exposure to extreme cold

gangrene a condition in which flesh dies; usually caused by a bad infection or large loss of blood

gasoline a type of fuel used in engines

glacier a large piece of ice that flows very slowly across land

navigator a person trained to use the sun and stars to find their way

paraffin an oily liquid used as fuel

pemmican a food mixture of dried meat and fat, sometimes with berries or other ingredients, that gives a person lots of energy

scurvy a disease caused by lack of vitamin C, which leads to bleeding gums and open wounds

snowdrift a mound of snow that is made by the wind

INDEX

READ MORE

Barone, Rebecca E.F. *Race to the Bottom of the Earth: Surviving Antarctica.* New York: Henry Holt and Co., 2021.

Eason, Sarah. *Arctic and Antarctic Survival Guide (Brave the Biome).* New York: Crabtree, 2021.

Micklos, John, Jr. *The Deadly Race to the South Pole (Deadly Expeditions).* North Mankato, MN: Capstone Press, 2022.

LEARN MORE ONLINE

1. Go to **www.factsurfer.com** or scan the QR code below.

2. Enter **"Death at South Pole"** into the search box.

3. Click on the cover of this book to see a list of websites.

Answers to the quiz on page 30
1) B; 2) C; 3) A; 4) B; 5) A